Gallery Books
Editor: Peter Fallon

PERFORMANCES

Brian Friel

PERFORMANCES

Gallery Books

Performances
is first published
simultaneously in paperback
and in a clothbound edition
on the day of its première,
30 September 2003.

The Gallery Press
Loughcrew
Oldcastle
County Meath
Ireland

ISBN 1 85235 354 6 (*paperback*)
1 85235 355 4 (*clothbound*)

A CIP catalogue record for this book
is available from the British Library.

    The Gallery Press acknowledges the financial assistance of An Chomhairle Ealaíon / The Arts Council, Ireland.

for Peter Fallon
friend and publisher

Characters

LEOŠ JANÁČEK, composer
ANEZKA UNGROVA, graduate student

Musicians
RUTH, first violin
JUDITH, second violin
MIRIAM, viola
JOHN, cello

Set
Janáček's work-room in Brno, capital of Moravia

Time
The present

Performances was first produced in the Gate Theatre, Dublin, on 30 September 2003, with the following cast:

LEOŠ JANÁČEK	Ion Caramitru
ANEZKA UNGROVA	Niamh Linehan
RUTH	Nicola Sweeney
JUDITH	Jana Ludvíčková
MIRIAM	Fay Sweet
DAVID	Tony Woollard
Director	Patrick Mason
Designer	Joe Vaněk
Lighting Designer	Paul Keogan

Nicola Sweeney, Jana Ludvíčková, Fay Sweet and Tony Woollard make up the Alba String Quartet whose performance of *Intimate Letters* is woven through the play.

I am indebted to Michael Colgan who introduced me to Janáček's letters to Kamila Stösslová and suggested there might be a play in them.

And I am indebted once again to George Steiner whose observations on composition and string quartets were invaluable to me.

— Brian Friel

Quotations from *Intimate Letters: Leoš Janáček to Kamila Stösslová*, edited and translated by John Tyrrell (1994), by kind permission of Faber and Faber.

Music

Pre-curtain: 'I'll Wait for You'. Piano.
'You Promised to Marry Me'. Piano. Played twice.
'On that Clear Field of Hurasky'. Piano.
'A Stream is Running'. Piano.
'On that Javorina Plain'. Piano.
Dvořák's *String Quartet in F-major*, Op.96 — finale — bars 38-84.
Janáček's *Second String Quartet* — third movement — bars 29-50. (The 'lullaby' sequence)
Janáček's *Second String Quartet* — first movement — first 9 bars.
'I'll Wait for You'. Piano.
Janáček's *Second String Quartet* — second movement — bars 1-11.
Janáček's *Second String Quartet* — second movement — the flautato ('nightingale') sextuplets.
Janáček's *Second String Quartet* — first two movements in full — offstage (approximately 12½ minutes). Final two movements in full — onstage (approximately 13½ minutes).

Piano music before the lights go down: 'I'll Wait for You'.
Curtain up.

JANÁČEK's *work-room in Brno, Moravia. The decor, fur-nishings, curtains etc are all in the style of the twenties. A functional, bachelor's room. A wood-burning stove, unlit. A piano stage right. (Right and left from the point of view of the audience.) The composer's work-table and chair stage left. A few chairs along the back wall. These will be used later by the musicians. Two chairs and two music-stands are already in position* — *one chair for the cellist, placed below the piano, and one chair for the first violinist, placed below the work-table. All four instruments* — *two violins, viola, cello* — *are onstage. On top of the piano a very large bowl of lettuce leaves. A large jug of water on a small table.* JANÁČEK *drinks from it frequently throughout the evening.*

JANÁČEK *wrote his* String Quartet No. 2 — Intimate Letters
as he called it — *over a period of three weeks in January/ February, 1928. He was then in his seventy-fourth year. He died on August 12, 1928.*

It becomes apparent very early that JANÁČEK *is long dead. It is important that he is played by an actor in his fifties or energetic sixties.*

JANÁČEK *is seated at the piano. He finishes the piano piece we have been listening to ('I'll Wait for You'), turns a few pages, begins another piece — 'You Promised to Marry Me'. He is a small man, plump and vigorous, with grey hair. He exudes vitality. He speaks rapidly, his mind leaping impatiently and with seeming illogic from one idea to the next. While* JANÁČEK *plays,* RUTH *arranges flowers in a vase. She is first violinist in the quartet. She is fully at ease in this house — as indeed are all the members of the quartet.*

RUTH Pretty, aren't they?

JANÁČEK Sorry?

RUTH Freesia. Aren't they pretty?

JANÁČEK Lovely. Are they your own?

RUTH Miriam's. She's a genius with flowers. Get her to show you around her garden some day.

JANÁČEK Is she here?

RUTH Just arrived. She's been to the dentist.

JANÁČEK Poor child. Does she feel like playing?

RUTH Of course she does. (*Looking around — housework finished*) Now. That's your fresh water.

JANÁČEK You're a saint.

RUTH That's true. And your fresh lettuce — Miriam's, too.

JANÁČEK An angel.

RUTH Also true. I might shampoo that carpet next week.

JANÁČEK The carpet's spotless. When are you going to play for me?

RUTH Ten minutes. John's making a pot of coffee. Do you want some?

JANÁČEK Coffee doesn't agree with me, Ruth. Don't you know that?

RUTH Forgot. Sorry — sorry. (*As she leaves*) Do you know that the sash-cord in that window is broken?

JANÁČEK The window is fine, thank you.

RUTH I could fix it for you.

JANÁČEK Thank you.

RUTH Take me no time at all.

JANÁČEK Out — out!

She leaves. He continues playing and turning pages.

Enter ANEZKA. *She is an anxious, intense and earnest young woman. She uses glasses for reading. She is in her late twenties, a student at Prague University where she is working on a Doctorate on Janáček's later work. Even though she is in awe of* JANÁČEK *she is very dogged in her questioning. Because she is late for her appointment, as she enters she is already pulling off her hat, coat and scarf. Eventually she will sit at the work-table, take her notes from her briefcase and spread them across the table. Janáček's letters, to which she constantly refers, are in a large, clip-folder with a distinctive bright green back.*

The moment she enters, JANÁČEK — *without interrupting his playing* — *challenges her. He moves on to another piece, 'On that Clear Field of Hurasky'.*

ANEZKA Forgive me, Mr Janáček, I —

JANÁČEK Late again.

ANEZKA What happened was —

JANÁČEK Second time, Anezka.

ANEZKA I know. I really *am* sorry.

JANÁČEK What was the catastrophe this time?

ANEZKA Power failure in Prague. So the computer system crashed. So the whole railway network is in chaos. No trains at all from Prague to Pisek and the connection from Jihlava to Brno here was over an hour —

He begins a new piece, 'A Stream is Running'.

JANÁČEK What's this?

ANEZKA I do apologise. And they wouldn't tell us how long we'd have to —

JANÁČEK (*Irritably*) The piece — the piece — what is it?

ANEZKA (*Immediately*) 'A Stream is Running' — from your Moravian Love Song collection of nineteen —

JANÁČEK Exactly. And this?

He plays 'On that Javorina Plain'.

ANEZKA (*Immediately*) 'On that Javorina Plain'.

JANÁČEK (*Surprised*) Exactly, Anezka!

ANEZKA Published by Hudebni matice in —

JANÁČEK I know when it was published, don't I? Twenty years after I was buried, for God's sake.

He leafs though the pages and plays casual arpeggios. As he does:

Do you find this room chilly?

ANEZKA I'm fine, thanks.

JANÁČEK I'd light the stove but the fumes aggravate my asthma. You'll have to forgive me, Anezka — I've forgotten your surname again.

ANEZKA Ungrova.

JANÁČEK Of course. Anezka Ungrova from Jihlava. Is there a man in your life?

ANEZKA (*Deeply embarrassed*) No — not at the moment — well, what I mean is not exactly a man.

He considers this briefly.

JANÁČEK What then?

ANEZKA What I mean is — not in the sense of somebody who —

JANÁČEK Should be. You're an attractive woman.

ANEZKA Thank you.
JANÁČEK Very attractive.
ANEZKA Actually there was somebody — four-and-a-half years ago — from Milan — visiting lecturer in Statistics — Orlando —
JANÁČEK (*Not listening*) Statistics? Beautiful . . .
ANEZKA Tiniest little man — with shy brown eyes . . .
JANÁČEK Not bad at all . . .
ANEZKA He used to say he was sometimes taken for a dwarf — because he was so tiny.
JANÁČEK Very nice too . . .
ANEZKA He wasn't, of course — a dwarf. Just . . . not tall. We corresponded for a full year after he left. Every day at least. Sometimes twice a day. Scores of letters. Hundreds. Then for some reason it all just seemed to fizzle —
JANÁČEK Must have spent years jotting down this silly stuff. (*Hums/sings*) Sort of musical doodles, aren't they? The Doodles of Leoš Janáček. Will they deserve a mention in your thesis? Footnote, maybe. The Joodles of Leoš Lanáček — The Loodles of Deoš Danáček. Ah! And this?

He plays bars 38-84 from the last movement of Dvořák's String Quartet in F-major, *Op.96.*

ANEZKA 'On a Black Mountain'.
JANÁČEK No.
ANEZKA Is it 'The Golden Ring'?
JANÁČEK No.
ANEZKA I know. From your opera *Káťa Kab* —
JANÁČEK Mine? Good God, no!
ANEZKA I'm lost.
JANÁČEK Mr Antonín Dvořák.
ANEZKA It's not, is it?
JANÁČEK Vigorous — as you would expect. Much too folksy-themes-and-dirndl-skirt for my taste.

ANEZKA There is a story that you bumped into Dvořák on your honeymoon and when —

JANÁČEK You'd never guess where he wrote this: a place called Spillville, Oh-hi-oh. Yes!

ANEZKA And when you introduced the new Mrs Janáček to him, he said, 'In the name of God, Leoš, you've married a child!'

JANÁČEK Some child! Fifteen-and-a-half, for God's sake! At least! You got that bit of tattle in the autobiography of Mrs Janáček.

ANEZKA Mr Janáček, I'd like to talk to you today about Kamila — if I may — Mrs Stösslová — Kamila Stösslová —

JANÁČEK Mrs Janáček was Morovia's supreme fantasist. You should be more rigorous with your sources, young lady.

ANEZKA And about the very special relationship you had with her — with Kamila.

JANÁČEK An American millionaire paid Dvořák's heirs two hundred thousand dollars for just six of his manuscripts. Isn't that astonishing? And that was eighty years ago!

ANEZKA Your biographers have all written of that relationship with Mrs Stösslová as one of the great love affairs.

JANÁČEK All the same, a great, great Slavic composer. Maybe the best of us. Certainly the most loved of us. But that's not quite the same thing, is it?

ANEZKA (*Persisting*) You did write her scores of letters, Mr Janáček. Hundreds. Very passionate letters indeed.

JANÁČEK And you should have heard his *Requiem* at my funeral service. It was . . . august. In the old Opera House where they had me lying in state. Curious expression that — 'lying in state' — isn't it?

He flexes the fingers of his right hand.

ANEZKA It is those letters I'd like to talk to you about today, Mr Janáček — if you wouldn't mind. Especially the letters you wrote to her almost at the end of your life when you were working on your Second String Quartet.

JANÁČEK What's keeping these people?

He goes to the door and shouts.

Anybody out there? (*To* ANEZKA) Got to do something about this arthritis. Knuckles are beginning to swell. Raw carrots, maybe?

RUTH *enters.*

RUTH We have fresh coffee out there — I know, Maestro.

JANÁČEK Well, should you ever get round to playing a little music . . .

RUTH Don't rush us. We're psyching ourselves up.

JANÁČEK 'Psyching ourselves —'! This is Anezka. Ruth. Anezka — Anezka — (*Slaps his forehead*) Gone!

ANEZKA Ungrova.

JANÁČEK Of course. Ruth is our first violinist with the quartet.

RUTH⎫
ANEZKA⎭ Hello — hello.

JANÁČEK And as well as being an accomplished fiddler Ruthie is a skilled do-it-yourself woman.

ANEZKA Really?

JANÁČEK So she believes. They come here to play now and again — just for a bit of fun. And the very persistent Ms Ungrova is doing a thesis on my later work.

RUTH Good!

ANEZKA I'm focussing on one year only — 1928.

RUTH The year of your Second String Quartet, Maestro — right?

ANEZKA That's what I'm working on — the Quartet!

RUTH Good for you!

JANÁČEK Not a bad year, was it?

RUTH It was a major year. Probably your most creative year ever.

ANEZKA The year he died, too.

JANÁČEK Anezka has her own . . . impish way of classifying events. When will you be adequately psyched up?

RUTH Ten minutes at most, Maestro. All right?

> *As soon as she enters and during the above exchanges* RUTH *removes her violin from its case. Very swiftly her fingers brush across the four strings — yes, they are in tune. And immediately she plays the first nine bars of the first movement of the* String Quartet No. 2. *Just as she finishes those nine bars,* JANÁČEK *plays the same nine bars, adding a full improvised piano accompaniment. Then, when* JANÁČEK *finishes,* RUTH *repeats the nine bars by herself.*

RUTH (*To* ANEZKA, *as she plays*) The opening of that Quartet.

ANEZKA Yes. The andante.

RUTH (*Sings*) Ta-ra-ra-ra — Ta-ra-ra-ra. 'I'm my own man', that's what it says to me.

ANEZKA (*Reads from the green folder*) 'I've just completed the opening movement and it is all about our first fateful encounter and how you instantly enslaved me —' Mr Janáček's letter to Kamila, February 1, 1928.

RUTH (*Indifferently*) Bang goes my little theory then, doesn't it?

JANÁČEK (*To* RUTH) She keeps producing these ridiculous quotations. (*To* ANEZKA) You invent them, Ms Ungrova, don't you?

ANEZKA It's your handwriting, Mr Janáček.

RUTH Let's move on. What about this?

RUTH *begins playing from the third movement, bars 29-50. The 'lullaby' sequence.*

ANEZKA The 'lullaby' sequence! From the third movement, the moderato! Am I right?

JANÁČEK You'd need to be on your toes here, Ruthie.

RUTH So it seems!

ANEZKA 'A slave, yes, but such a happy, divinely happy slave. But there are no words to talk of a meeting like that. So I talk about it in the andante.'

JANÁČEK Anezka missed the train this morning — power failure at Prague Central. So the computer collapsed.

RUTH You're from Prague?

ANEZKA Jihlava. It's between Pisek and Brno.

JANÁČEK Why not play in here, Ruth? The acoustic's sharper. Bit chilly though, isn't it?

RUTH I don't think so. (*Mock concern*) But don't you take any risks with that chest of yours. (*To* ANEZKA) He's not all that robust.

JANÁČEK Ruthie!

RUTH Sorry, Maestro.

ANEZKA May I have a coffee?

RUTH Certainly may. We'll have a warm-up before we join you.

She exits with her violin.

JANÁČEK Love having them about. They fill the house with brio.

RUTH (*Head around the door*) Maybe I could fix that

computer?

JANÁČEK Out! (*Head disappears*) She's irrepressible, Ruth.

> *Pause. Then, in an embarrassed but determined rush* —

ANEZKA Mr Danáček, I really would like to talk about these (*letters*) —

JANÁČEK Danáček?

ANEZKA Oh my God — forgive me, Mr Janáček — you have me all confused — I really am sorry —

JANÁČEK Call me . . . Mr Doodle?

ANEZKA Yes — very funny — yes — but would you agree — before the musicians join us — would you perhaps consent to talk about the relationship between that quartet and the love letters you wrote to Mrs Stösslová when you were working on it — or would you consider that a little too intrusive — perhaps?

JANÁČEK A little too vulgar — perhaps? A new American musical came to Brno here that same January of 1928. 'No, No, Nanette'. And it had a song called (*Sings*) 'I want to be happy but I won't be happy'. Like an evangelical hymn, isn't it? Anyhow, for months after they left, *that's* what the whole of Brno was singing. Not Leoš Janáček, I'm afraid.

ANEZKA I did scruple over this, Mr Janáček: is it an area of honest exploration or is it just vulgar curiosity? And I came to the conclusion that it is totally honest.

JANÁČEK Well scrupled. Congratulations.

ANEZKA Because there must be a connection between the private life and the public work, Mr Janáček.

JANÁČEK Must there?

ANEZKA Oh yes. Don't you think so? And I believe a full appreciation of the quartet isn't possible unless *all* the circumstances of its composition are considered — and that must include an analysis of your emotional state at that time — and these letters provide significant evidence about that.

JANÁČEK Mightn't this kind of naïve scrutiny have frightened off your little statistician? — (*Instant regret*) Apologies.

ANEZKA In fact that is really the core of my thesis, Mr Janáček: the relationship between the writing of that piece and those passionate letters from a seventy-four-year-old man to a woman almost forty years younger than him — a married woman with two young sons — and what I hope to suggest is that your passion for Kamila Stösslová certainly had a determining effect on that composition and indeed on that whole remarkable burst of creative energy at the very end of your life — probably caused it, for heaven's sake — and only six months away from your death!

JANÁČEK Known by the rabble as the condemned man's final erection as he mounts the scaffold. And this 'only six months away' — is this mischievous count-down necessary?

ANEZKA And I will try to show that when you wrote this quartet — '*Intimate Letters*' — you call it that yourself when you were head-over-heels in love with her — my thesis will demonstrate that the Second String Quartet is a textbook example of a great passion inspiring a great work of art and it will prove that work of art to be the triumphant apotheosis of your entire creative life.

JANÁČEK Gracious me!

ANEZKA And I intend to draw parallels between your story and the story of the other classical passions — Dante and Beatrice — Petrarch and Laura — and I must confess to you, Mr Janáček — I have got to tell you it is a story that breaks my heart into tiny fragments and at the same time sends it soaring exultantly.

JANÁČEK Poor abused heart!

ANEZKA (*Delving into the letters*) Bear with me for another second, Mr Janáček, please. 'I have just finished the adagio' — that's the second movement —

JANÁČEK Really?

ANEZKA Exactly. 'And it is all about you, my sun, my galaxy of stars, and how our very first meeting set my soul ablaze with the most exquisite melodies. And this will be *our* composition because it will be quick with our passion, and our mutual love will bear it in glory up into the heavens.'

JANÁČEK Along with your abused heart.

ANEZKA Then, when you begin the third movement —

JANÁČEK The moderato.

ANEZKA Exactly, Mr Janáček — you write to tell her about the lullaby you are weaving into it — Ruth just played it — a haunting filigree theme repeated twice — 'because I want to hint at the idea of motherhood' — that's something you keep coming back to — motherhood — Kamila pregnant with the child of your passion — 'so that the work will be seen as the consummation of all our desires'. Freudian crap — pardon me — but deeply, deeply moving.

JANÁČEK That at least. Now take a deep breath and listen to this, Anezka.

ANEZKA Then, when you come to the final movement —

JANÁČEK The allegro.

ANEZKA Exactly, Mr Janáček — then you wrote to Kamila: 'The last movement is charged with energy and defiance. But it is a movement without fear; just a great longing and some-

thing like a fulfilment of that longing.' Don't
quite understand that 'defiance'.

JANÁČEK (*Quietly*) Listen.

ANEZKA 'I am calling the piece *Intimate Letters*. And as I
wrote it I trembled with such joy, such happi-
ness, that every bar is a proclamation of my
desire for you because my whole creative life
takes its heartbeat from you.'

JANÁČEK May I, Anezka?

ANEZKA 'Because you, Kamila, Kamila my love, you are
my very essence and without you I cannot exist.'
The work and the life! Inextricable! Indistinguishable! Identical! (*Softly*) I'm sorry, Mr
Janáček. I get a little bit . . . I just find it all so . . .

JANÁČEK Listen to this.

ANEZKA Sorry.

JANÁČEK This is the last thing I ever wrote.

ANEZKA (*Excited again*) In your holiday house! In Hukvaldy!

JANÁČEK In Hukvaldy.

He begins playing 'I'll Wait for You'.

ANEZKA You and Kamila were alone there — at last!

JANÁČEK (*Quietly*) We were. Yes. A time of frenzy. Violence
even. Despair too. And then when all that
ferment was about to overwhelm me — a few
minutes of sudden peace — no longer — an
amnesty sent from above maybe; and this
fragment came to me, a little melodic tendril.
Trivial, I know. But I remember placing those
limpid notes on the page with such care, so
delicately, as if they were fragile. And I remember thinking: simplicity like this, innocence like
this, that's closer to the heart of it, isn't it? —
That's what you should have listened for all
your life and not now at the frantic end. It stops

in mid-sentence. Listen. (*He illustrates*) Almost with expectation, as if it were holding its breath for a conclusion to be offered. And I remember thinking: if he could sing, maybe Adam sang something like this to his Eve. (*Laughs*) Or maybe, Anezka, maybe it wasn't simplicity at all. Maybe at that point the old composer was finally threadbare. And he called it 'I'll Wait for You'. Silly title: his time had run out by then.

ANEZKA No, no, you're wrong. You didn't die for another —

JANÁČEK Being grisly again? You're right, of course: he did love her.

ANEZKA Over seven hundred letters, Mr Janáček. I know so well.

JANÁČEK Adored her — so he told himself.

ANEZKA Such a pity she insisted you destroy most of her letters to you.

> JANÁČEK *jumps to his feet. He is suddenly brisk again.*

JANÁČEK Forever vigilant of her good name. A slave to small-town tyrannies. Anyhow, writing letters — for God's sake, writing a grocery list — sent her into a panic. (*Whispers*) Between ourselves — practically illiterate. (*Aloud*) As for my music, what I was reaching for — altogether beyond her sympathies. What you must understand is that Mrs Stösslová was a woman of resolute . . . ordinariness. Wasn't he a real pig!

ANEZKA I just *know* you did love her.

JANÁČEK But that's what you're thinking, isn't it? Aren't all artists users? If I sit too long I get a pain in this leg. Artery trouble. That's where it all began (*heart*). Have some lettuce. I live on lettuce and water ever since that bout of shingles. Miraculous stuff. What's keeping these people?

Enter JOHN *and* JUDITH, *both laughing.* JUDITH *carries a cup of coffee.*

JOHN Here we are! You'd never believe what that woman has just said.

JUDITH I spoke the truth.

JOHN 'With my perfect bowing technique and my beautiful hair any quartet in the world would kill to have me.'

JUDITH Just tell him it's true, Maestro.

JANÁČEK Absolutely true, John.

JOHN She's off her head! She's taking something! What are you on, Judith?

JUDITH Who's the coffee for?

ANEZKA Me, I think.

JANÁČEK Anezka from Jihlava.

JOHN Ruthie told us. You're the PhD.

ANEZKA Not yet, I'm afraid. Everything will depend on how I handle these (*letters*).

JANÁČEK John is the cellist and Judith is second fiddle.

JOHN
JUDITH Hello — hello — hello.
ANEZKA

JUDITH We're all here now, Maestro. Miriam's back from the dentist.

JANÁČEK Is she all right?

JUDITH A bit weepy but she's fine.

JOHN (*Privately to* ANEZKA) I gave her a triple vodka.

JUDITH *picks up her violin and plays the first eleven bars of the opening of the second movement, the adagio.*

JANÁČEK (*To* ANEZKA) The beginning of the second movement.

ANEZKA The adagio.

JANÁČEK Exactly.

JOHN (*To* ANEZKA) I just adore her hair, don't you?

JUDITH Stop it, John!

JANÁČEK Tell you what you'll do, Judith. Skip ahead to those descending sextuplets — that flautato figure — and we'll see how smart our Doctor is. (*To* ANEZKA) I wrote these sounds into my notebook one day when we were out walking in the woods — yes, in Hukvaldy.

> JUDITH *plays the flautato.*

Kamila identified the song immediately. She was very good at birds. Well?

ANEZKA Well what?

JANÁČEK What bird *is* it?

ANEZKA (*Immediately*) A nightingale.

JANÁČEK Clever!

JUDITH Well done, Anezka.

JANÁČEK A nightingale in mourning, a lamenting nightingale.

> JOHN *plays the same flautato figure — very slowly and woozily.*

JOHN And that, Maestro?

JANÁČEK (*To* ANEZKA) They're comedians, too. (*To* JOHN) All right, what is it?

JOHN The same mourning nightingale on the way home from the pub.

JANÁČEK Out — out — out!

> JOHN *and* JUDITH *leave with their instruments. They pause at the door.*

JOHN   Don't worry about Miriam, Maestro. All she
       had done was a routine check-up.
JUDITH   She's sobbing out there, John!
JOHN   Nerves. She began sobbing last Monday.

They leave — laughing.

JANÁČEK   Where would I be without their company?
          They're my life-support group.

> JANÁČEK *picks up the loose piano sheets and
> busily arranges them.* ANEZKA *goes to him with
> the green folder.*

ANEZKA   May I get back to these, Mr Janáček?
JANÁČEK   Sorry?
ANEZKA   The letters — the Second Quartet.
JANÁČEK   These pieces (*Piano*) were never properly cata-
          logued until years after I was dead.
ANEZKA   They tell us so much about your working
         methods, too.
JANÁČEK   It was almost five years since the First Quartet
          and I remember I was terrified tackling that
          complex architecture again, probably the most
          intricate structure a man can put together.
ANEZKA   You don't talk to her of any terror.
JANÁČEK   That labyrinth of interweaving melodies; finding
          the exact interaction of feelings and meanings;
          getting the precise balance between a statement
          and its qualification, maybe even its denial. For
          God's sake, do you think she would have under-
          stood anything of that?
ANEZKA   But you do write again and again about the
         great joy and excitement of composing.
JANÁČEK   I wrote what she might possibly comprehend.

The door bursts open and MIRIAM *dashes in and*

grabs her viola. She holds a handkerchief to her jaw.

MIRIAM Sorry — sorry — sorry — can't speak — beg your pardon —
JANÁČEK Are you all right, Miriam?
MIRIAM Yes — thanks — fine — fine — really — back soon —
JANÁČEK Thank you for the freesia, Miriam. And the lettuce. Beautiful.

But she has exited with her viola.

Miriam's our viola. Probably is only nerves. What do you think?
ANEZKA Probably. The letters, Mr Janáček; the Second String Quartet.
JANÁČEK The Second String Quartet. Facing that mountain again? — of course I was terrified. And then there was that other fear: will the seventy-four-year-old body have the stamina to keep up with this (*head*)? — To marshal this ferment?

Offstage the quartet begins playing the String Quartet *from the top.*

There they go. 'I'm my own man' — I don't think it says that. More a whistle in the dark, isn't it?
ANEZKA (*Reads*) 'Today the Moravian String Quartet came to play the first two movements. First time ever played! I was very nervous. But they were so enthusiastic. They insisted they'd never heard music like it.' May 18, just three months before your death.
JANÁČEK (*To himself*) Why *does* the woman do that?
ANEZKA 'I don't think I am capable of writing anything more profound or more truthful. This quartet

29

might have been cut out of my living flesh.'

JANÁČEK I never wrote that!

ANEZKA 'Before this I composed from emotions remembered, out of feeling recollected in perfect calm.'

JANÁČEK That's true. (*Laughs*) Pinched that line from some English poet. Name's gone, too.

ANEZKA 'But with this quartet, my *Intimate Letters* to you, my love, I wrote from feelings experienced directly and vividly. This was composed in fire out of the furnace that is our great love.'

JANÁČEK (*Listening*) Not bad though, is it?

ANEZKA And two days later: 'And what can I tell you of that great love that inspired this work? It is a fire that boils like strong wine' —

JANÁČEK 'Boils like strong —!' God!

ANEZKA 'And where did it come from, this inextinguishable flame?'

JANÁČEK William Wordsworth — 'emotions recollected'! Where did *that* come from?

ANEZKA 'From your deep enigmatic eyes; from every curve of your exquisite body; from the glow of your radiant black hair.'

JANÁČEK Curious. Why do I remember it as mousy?

ANEZKA And later on that same day: 'A play called *Cyrano de Bergerac* opened here in Brno last week. About a man who pours out his passion for the woman he loves in a series of love letters. And in the last act he dies of a mortal wound. Will that be my fate?'

JANÁČEK Wrong in the detail. Not of a wound. Diseased aorta. I told you — began here (*Taps his leg*). Then cardiac failure. (*Listening*) God, aren't they good!

ANEZKA Actually, according to the post-mortem report . . . I know it says something here about pneumonia —

JANÁČEK Anezka, my dear, you'd learn so much more by

just listening to the music.

Silence. They listen.

Did I say not bad? It's damned good.

ANEZKA The day that the Moravian String Quartet played the first two movements — here in this room — you wrote to Kamila that they were 'bowled over' by it.

JANÁČEK 'Bowled over' — 'cut out of my living flesh' — 'boiling wine' — you're making this up, aren't you?

ANEZKA All here.

JANÁČEK Thank God my first language was music. And a much more demanding language it is, too.

ANEZKA Is it?

JANÁČEK Oh yes. Because we reach into that amorphous world of feeling and sing what we hear in the language of feeling itself; a unique vocabulary of sounds created by feeling itself.

ANEZKA You did that there, Mr Janáček.

JANÁČEK The people who huckster in words merely report on feeling. We *speak* feeling. I remember when I finished it I really thought that — yes! — this time I had solved the great paradox: had created something that was singular to me, uniquely mine, bearing the imprint of my spirit only; and at the same time was made new again in every listener who was attentive and assented to its strange individuality and to its arrogance and indeed to its hesitancies. (*Laughs*) Vanity. That's what distance lends: clarity. You'll learn that in time, too, Anezka. I promise you.

ANEZKA Mr Janáček, I'd like to ask you about one particular letter.

JANÁČEK Sure you're not cold?

ANEZKA I'm fine. Dated July 9, 1924. A few days after your seventieth birthday. May I quote it?

JANÁČEK I could light a small fire?

ANEZKA It's one of the few surviving letters from Kamila to you. If I may.

JANÁČEK Why does that humble 'if I may' always put me on guard? (*Listens*) Working with musicians of that calibre is so satisfying for a composer.

ANEZKA You had stayed overnight in Pisek with her husband, David, and herself — remember that?

JANÁČEK Go on.

ANEZKA 'I was glad that I seen you and heard your conversation and you and me and David were all so happy and had such good innocent fun together and the picnic was lovely and the time just flew didn't it.'

JANÁČEK What a jolly school outing. (*Listens*) God, they *are* talented.

ANEZKA 'And to think there was a time when I didn't even want to talk to you and here I am writing to you when I should be ironing my David's shirts — oh my.'

JANÁČEK 'Oh my'. Oh dear!

ANEZKA And she finishes off with this — this — perhaps it is a little insensitive — No, it's not important.

JANÁČEK Read it.

ANEZKA No, it hasn't anything to do with —

JANÁČEK For God's sake, read it.

ANEZKA 'And it *is* all very innocent because you could be my father no I am wrong you could be my grandfather and that is why my David always calls you Grandpa Jana to give the boys a good laugh and do you think I would ever dream of writing to you at all if you weren't a very old man because if you weren't, my husband, David, would certainly put an end to it very quick and then . . .'

A little gauche the way she . . . Of course she loves you. But she's reminding you she's a married woman with two small boys and maybe she's suggesting, too — as gently as she can — that perhaps you're not in love with her but with an imagined Kamila, an image of her you've fashioned yourself. I know she doesn't intend to wound. Just expresses herself clumsily. I know very well how easily that can be done. And all the regrets that follow on. You said yourself she had no talent for putting her thoughts on paper.

JANÁČEK Grocery thoughts — with effort.

ANEZKA The important thing is that you were able to absorb it because your love for her was so — so copious. That really is the important thing. I do know that.

JANÁČEK What you're suggesting — not so gently — is that I was a ridiculous old fool?

ANEZKA A — ? Oh God no, Mr Janáček! Not at all! The very opposite! Yes, yes, she's saying: slow down — cautious — could be difficulties here. And how do you respond? An outpouring of even more passionate letters! Reaffirmations of your devotion! An enormous deluge of love! And that must have been so reassuring for her! And that was so courageous, so *faithful* of you! I think your response was just noble, Mr Janáček. I think you were . . . august.

She covers her face in her hands in acute embarrassment at her outburst.

I'm sorry. I've no right to speak to you like that.

JANÁČEK *stands very still, hearing only the music.*

33

Pause.

Forgive me.

JANÁČEK That's no image. That's the real thing.

ANEZKA What I was trying to say —

JANÁČEK The thing realized. The aspiration fulfilled. All you have in those stammering pages are dreams of music, desires for the dream sounds in the head. And in those stammering pages those aspirations — desires — dreams — they're transferred on to a perfectly decent but quite untutored young woman. And in time the distinction between his dreams and that young woman became indistinguishable, so that in his head she was transformed into something immeasurably greater — of infinitely more importance — than the quite modest young woman she was, in fact. Indeed in time he came to see her — miraculously — as the achieved thing itself! The music in the head made real, become carnal! Came to know no distinction between the dream music and the dream woman! Foolish old man. (*Listens, smiling, to the music off*) Yes.

ANEZKA (*Total shock*) You're teasing me, Mr Janáček — aren't you?

JANÁČEK By the way, he never did possess her — not that that matters. And that (*music off*) is the closest he ever got to the dream sounds in the head. But to have got that close, I suppose Kamila has to be acknowledged . . . 'perhaps'?

ANEZKA You can't mean that you —?

JANÁČEK And it's not surprising he loved her, is it? After all, he had invented her as an expression of what was the very best in himself, hadn't he?

ANEZKA (*Incredulous*) Oh, Mr Janáček, you —

JANÁČEK Look at that disapproving face! Yes — yes —

yes — a real pig, I know.

ANEZKA (*Real question*) How dare you, Mr Janáček? How dare you?

JANÁČEK Did no one ever tell you you're far too pale? Go on a lettuce diet. It's more than restorative — it's regenerative. Incidentally, a little nugget for your thesis: I wrote dozens of lullabies. None of the biographers knows that. Began just after my son was born — Vladimir.

ANEZKA I was in awe of you, Mr Janáček: you were endowed so uniquely, so exceptionally privileged, I really believed you were . . . chosen.

JANÁČEK We called him Vladicek — my son. Pet name. Died when he was just two. And every year for the next forty years I wrote a lullaby for him on his birthday. And burned it. Lullabies tend to be sentimental, don't they?

ANEZKA And what you have just said just — just — just stuns me.

JANÁČEK Really?

ANEZKA What you have just said about Kamila — I must object very strongly, Mr Janáček.

JANÁČEK Oh my.

ANEZKA Suddenly those three years have turned to . . . vapour.

The four members of the quartet enter with their instruments, set up their music stands and prepare to play.

RUTH We decided to play the last two movements in here. What do you think?

JANÁČEK Why not? How are you, Miriam?

MIRIAM Fine, thanks.

JOHN Just being brave. She had a *very* rigorous checkup. You're looking energetic today, Maestro.

JANÁČEK Am I?

35

RUTH   That was the wrong thing to say.

JANÁČEK   I heard that! (*To* ANEZKA) Where will you and I sit?

ANEZKA   Anywhere.

JANÁČEK   This all right?

ANEZKA   Anywhere.

JANÁČEK   We're finished, aren't we?

ANEZKA   Yes.

JANÁČEK   You should pick up that correspondence again with your little Italian statistician. Here's a tip: have an image in your head of a tall, blond Swede.

ANEZKA   (*Angry, but controlled*) What you have just said about Kamila was a disgraceful thing to say, Mr Janáček.

JANÁČEK   Yes?

ANEZKA   That you transformed an unsophisticated young woman into something 'immeasurably greater, infinitely more important'. How dare you, Mr Janáček!

JANÁČEK   (*Innocently*) But I did, didn't I? Only in my head, of course.

ANEZKA   And cruel and heartless and deeply misogynistic.

JANÁČEK   Must I apologise again?

ANEZKA   Because I can tell you that the woman in these letters remained the dignified and 'perfectly agreeable' young woman she always was, despite your assaults on her life.

JANÁČEK   (*Mock alarm*) Assaults?

ANEZKA   Notes — gifts — the sudden visits — the relentless bombardment of letters that must have left the woman's head addled. So she was flattered by the attention of the famous composer and of course she responded. But was it really all that flattering to be looked on as an 'image' or the dream music made 'carnal'?

JANÁČEK To use your own elegant phrase — more Freudian crap?

ANEZKA I'm not competent to talk about your creative process and this is the only language I have to talk about what I know very well, intimately even. But I believe you did love Kamila Stösslová after a fashion — or at least as generously as your self-centred life permitted. Because that's what your letters proclaim, Mr Janáček, explicitly and repeatedly.

JANÁČEK I think I've said so, haven't I?

ANEZKA And I believe she loved you as fully and as generously as the conventions of her life allowed — 'tyrannies', if you prefer.

JANÁČEK But Dante and Beatrice? Hardly!

ANEZKA And to shut out that love from the story of your lives or to talk about it just as a metaphor for your composing process, that diminishes you, Mr Janáček, and it certainly runs contrary to the great amplitude of the Quartet. Of course it triumphs without these stammering pages. But knowing them enriches our intimacy with the work and how we 'assent' to it.

JANÁČEK I never considered the life all that important. I gave myself to the perfection of the work. Did I make the wrong choice?

ANEZKA Crap.

JANÁČEK Of course.

ANEZKA And in your withered heart you know it's crap. And I'd suggest, if I may, that you listen to the music again, too. And this time with all the open-mindedness and simplicity you claimed you once sought so eagerly, and you'll hear that love, too.

RUTH Any time you're ready, Maestro.

JANÁČEK (*To* ANEZKA) The Doctor is a little peeved, is she?

RUTH Are we right?

ANEZKA (*To* ALL) I'm sorry I have to rush off.

JOHN No, you don't.

ANEZKA Last train to catch.

RUTH I'll walk you to the station.

ANEZKA I'm really sorry.

JOHN Hold on. This lasts less than fifteen minutes.

RUTH John!

ANEZKA I'm really sorry. But I did hear the first two movements — wonderful. Thank you all. (*Formally to* JANÁČEK) And thank you for all your help.

JANÁČEK Welcome.

ANEZKA I'll write you next week.

JANÁČEK A very punctilious thank-you letter — I know.

She leaves the green folder beside him.

ANEZKA I'm sure they *are* full of metaphorical meaning, Mr Janáček. But I know, too, they can be read as the beautiful love letters they are.

JANÁČEK Thank you.

ANEZKA And I believe *that* reading is the truer reading.

JANÁČEK Not truer, Anezka. No, no, not truer. Yes, both readings can coexist — why not? Be held in a kind of equilibrium. Even be seen to illuminate one another. But finally, Anezka, finally — all this petty agitation aside (*green folder*) — the work's the thing. That must be insisted on. Everything has got to be ancillary to the work. And for all her naïvete in these matters even Kamila acknowledged the primacy of the work. She understood that from the very beginning: the work came first. And good for her! Eminently sensible Kamila! Pisek granite! (*Laughs*) Small-town granite, but granite all the same. And I think that tells us so much more about Mrs Stösslová than all this . . . excess.

ANEZKA *moves toward the door.*

RUTH 'Bye, Anezka.

ANEZKA 'Bye. 'Bye, all.

JOHN Will we see you again?

ANEZKA I hope so.

MIRIAM I hope so, too.

> ANEZKA *returns to* JANÁČEK *and speaks softly, intensely to him.*

ANEZKA I just know you're wrong, Mr Janáček. Every fibre in my body insists you're wrong. You don't know what the real thing is. This (*green folder*) is it. Indeed you couldn't be more wrong.

> *She leaves.*

JUDITH Nice lady.

MIRIAM Lovely lady.

JOHN (*To* MIRIAM) What about another vodka?

RUTH Come on! You can chat later. Work — work — work!

JUDITH Play — play — play!

> *The quartet begins playing the last two movements, the moderato and the allegro.*
>
> *For a long time* JANÁČEK *stares after the departed* ANEZKA. *Then he spots the green folder that she has left behind — should he call her back? He picks it up. Very slowly he turns it over in his hands and glances occasionally at the musicians. Now he opens the book and slowly and gently leafs through it, pausing now and then to read a line or two. Now he leans his head back and closes his eyes.*
>
> *Black-out the moment the allegro ends.*